Understanding an Atheist

A Practical Guide to
Relating to Nonbelievers

Second edition

KEVIN DAVIS

Copyright © 2017 SecularVoices Books

All rights reserved.

ISBN-10: **0692954260**
ISBN-13: **978-0692954263**

DEDICATION

To my wife Shannon, my best friend and number one fan, who continues to stand by me and support me, regardless of what crazy idea I present to her.

And to my sons Ryan and Grayson, who may one day read this book to better understand their religion-free childhood and appreciate their freedom to choose whichever belief systems will bring them happiness.

CONTENTS

	Foreword	i
1	Purpose	1
2	No Choice	7
3	The Journey	21
4	Coming Out	31
5	In the Open	41
6	What It Means	53
7	Changing Perceptions	65
8	Moving Forward	73
9	Experiences Shared	79

FOREWORD

By Faisal Saeed Al Mutar
Founder, Global Secular Humanist Movement

We live in very interesting but difficult times. The religiously unaffiliated minority is now the fastest growing demographic in the U.S., driven by a large number of young people identifying as nonreligious. I believe that improved connectivity and easy access to information has played a major role in this growth. A case can also be made for the idea that industrialism and the cultural diversity of big cities can cause someone to water down his or her traditional beliefs or reject them altogether. But in other parts of the world, especially the Middle East where I grew up, we are witnessing a huge rise of religious extremism, including prosecution and sometimes death to those who hold a minority view or what can be considered a heretical view. Currently in 13 countries around the world, all of them Muslim, people who openly espouse atheism or reject the official state religion of Islam face execution under the law.

In Iraq, my country of birth, atheism is not considered a crime. But considering that there is almost no functional government there, militias often take matters into their own hands and kill anyone who holds a different or more moderate ideology than them.

Things have to change, and the best way to begin is to

start a dialogue between those who have faith in the supernatural and those who don't. This dialogue has to be healthy in a way that both sides try to listen and understand each other's point of view without looking at each other as inferior human beings. Instead, we must view each other as equals under the law but with different beliefs and ideas about the purpose of life and the origin of the cosmos.

I am not in any sense saying that all beliefs are equally valid, nor am I advocating for moral and cultural relativism of any sort. At the same time, we have to examine, discuss, and even criticize each other's beliefs without attacking each other personally, and I think we can do that.

People of faith, along with atheists, agnostics and freethinkers, should join together in rejecting all forms of violence and speak out against all who try to use their ideology to deny others of basic human rights.

Understanding an Atheist is a book that aims to create that bridge of discussion, written from the perspective of a person that everyone can relate to. People like Kevin Davis, me, and many others who are nonbelievers, are human beings like everyone else. We love some and dislike others. Some of us want a family, some of us don't. Some of us are disciplined hard workers, and others value something different.

Atheism is not a system of beliefs or morality. It's simply a lack of theism. But atheism can many times serve as a basis for Humanistic morality, where decisions are compassion and reason-based, not authoritarian based. Atheists don't acknowledge the existence of a heaven or hell, or a need for them as concepts – they don't believe that a supernatural system of awards and punishments is needed to make moral decisions and be a good person.

I hope you will enjoy the book and the testimonies as much as I did, and that after reading *Understanding an Atheist*, you will be prepared to participate in the dialogue that needs to happen.

1

PURPOSE

"It's a strange myth that atheists have nothing to live for. It's the opposite. We have nothing to die for. We have everything to live for."

-Ricky Gervais

Atheist.

The word alone conjures up feelings of discontent in most, especially for those who were instructed throughout their lives that atheists are hell-bound sinners who reject God and hate him so deeply that they deny his existence altogether. Many believers have been taught various things throughout their lives about atheists: they've been misled, haven't been introduced to the "real Jesus," are pawns of Satan, or are actual antichrists on a mission to destroy souls and cast doubt in good religious people's minds. Some are even told that atheists are fake or an illusion, and that "There are no atheists in foxholes." To these individuals, atheists are lost souls in denial who must be shown the way through Jesus Christ.

Atheists are none of the above. I know this because I am one, and have been for over 20 years. Atheists are regular people, in most ways no different from the religious, who have come to different conclusions about the unexplained than believers have. The word "atheist" has been looked upon so negatively by the religious throughout the years that even many atheists don't care for it. There's a palpable stigma attached to the word so great that many who fit the category would more quickly call themselves agnostic, humanist, non-theist, freethinker, or even the newly popular "none," referring to the box one would check off on a survey regarding religious affiliation.

It's this perception of atheists that keeps many in the closet, afraid to come out to their families and friends for fear of ostracism. Instead, the closeted atheist attends church when asked, avoids the topic of religion in general, and prays alongside family members before dinner, fitting in to keep the peace -- going along to get along. It's the same type of behavior pattern we would see from a closeted homosexual: making remarks about the opposite sex when required, avoiding the relationship question altogether, and keeping quiet when the subject of LGBTQ equality is discussed. In fact, some gay atheist friends of mine have said that coming out as an atheist was much more difficult than coming out as gay, since recent shifts in societal acceptance have started to swing in favor of the LGBTQ community.

The stigma that accompanies atheism creates an uncomfortable barrier between believers and nonbelievers. Religious people will sometimes hide their beliefs in front of known atheists in order to avoid potential conflict or show sensitivity to the beliefs (or lack of) of the other. Conversely, an atheist may hide his atheism from the religious for the same reasons, or just to avoid being looked down upon or snickered at. This barrier can develop into a taboo around not discussing religion, which evolves into a lack of communication and understanding.

The purpose of this book is to assist and encourage those who believe in a supreme being to keep the lines of communication open with their nonbelieving friends or family members. As an out of the closet atheist, I've experienced the uncomfortable "elephant in the room" feeling when the topic of religion surfaces among loved ones who have been religious their entire lives. I have seen the eye rolls, I've heard the sighs, and I've felt the stares from others who look at me differently than they once did when I was a believer. It's easy to have negative reactions to such treatment, resulting in a mutual communication cut off and a widening gap filled with unrest and discomfort at family functions, especially those with religious significance – weddings, baptisms, funerals and the like. And over the years I've come to realize that it all stems from an avoidance of discussion and a lack of understanding that affects both sides of the religious impasse. Unless it's thoughtfully examined by both sides, it's impossible to understand the perspective of each.

UNDERSTANDING AN ATHEIST

What is it like to be an atheist?

What challenges do atheists face?

What is it like to have an atheist family member or friend?

What challenges do religious people face when in the presence of nonbelievers?

These are questions that should be examined in order to gain a mutual understanding of what each side faces. The problem is, more often than not, these conversations don't happen due to the predicted discomfort that will arise from such a discussion. And if they do happen, they're likely to cause more conflict, especially when both sides are passionate about their beliefs and less willing to offer up an open mind to the perspective of the other.

In the coming chapters, I'd like to share my journey in order to help those who believe in a higher power understand the experience of loved ones with an opposite point of view on the existence of a deity. You'll learn about my Catholic upbringing, multiple searches for truth and my own identity, becoming a "saved" Christian, coming to terms with my own doubts and atheism, and the reactions and feelings of my friends and family members.

In this text, I'll make several generalizations about the

religious (namely Christian) and the nonreligious. This is not because I feel members of each group are all the same and should be lumped together, but in my experience some general conclusions can be made that represent the majority of both groups. There will always be those who don't fit the mold, and I know that. It's impossible to understand what makes everyone tick simply based on their faith or lack thereof, so keep in mind that the generalizations are just that – representations of the people I've come in contact with throughout my trek from religion to freethought. My hope is that the story I share will help you better relate to the atheist in your life and break down communication barriers when it comes to the topic of religion.

After all, discussing religion among friends and family is only taboo if you deem it so.

2

NO CHOICE

"Clearly the person who accepts the Church as an infallible guide will believe whatever the Church teaches."

-Saint Thomas Aquinas

Without a doubt, the success of religious institutions hinges on children. In many religions, especially Christianity, children are brought into the fold as early as possible, through baptism, Sunday school, Bible camps, and many other youth-focused activities. The reason for this is pretty simple. Young children are impressionable. They still believe in magic. They trust adults and believe what they're told. They don't have the knowledge, experience, or means to challenge what they're being taught. It works.

Christian evangelists often cite the 4-14 window.[1] This refers to the impressionable years between the ages of four and fourteen, when children are more likely to believe what they're taught by their elders about religion and less likely to question it. During this span, kids are drawn toward faith groups by community

---

[1] https://en.wikipedia.org/wiki/Child_evangelism_movement

members and asked to commit their lives to Jesus, and in turn, asked to evangelize to their school classmates to steer them toward Christianity as well.

While most parents think they're doing the right thing for their children by enrolling them in religious activities, in the eyes of the nonreligious, they may be doing their kids a disservice. Instead of teaching children *how* to think, they are being taught *what* to think. This is something that irks many atheists to the core, especially those who come from a religious past. Childhood indoctrination is often mentioned in the same breath as child abuse by the nonbeliever.

If you're religious, you may be thinking, "OK, here comes the religion bashing. Why am I reading this?"

I understand that comparing Sunday school to child abuse may sound harsh or unfair especially since the intent of sending children through religious instruction is usually in line with doing what's best for them. But remember, the point here is to help the religious reader understand the point of view of their atheist loved ones. It's not my intent to offend, but instead, to inform and explain, so bear with me as I attempt to do that.

Imagine being 6 years old and led to a classroom inside your church, a place where you feel safe, normally accompanied by your family, surrounded by friends and neighbors and trusted church elders. In this classroom you're taught stories derived from the Bible, which are massaged to the point of being palatable to children. But at the heart of stories like Noah's Ark, Adam and Eve, and David and Goliath, are widespread death, war, and eternal punishment. Those elements are still present in the stories and touched upon, but largely glossed over.

Kids are attracted to the story of Noah's Ark because of the colorful imagery and pictures of animals. If asked what the story contains, they'll recall all the animals they can think of, walking onto a huge wooden boat, two by two. They'll describe a rainstorm and a massive flood, followed by a rainbow and a dove delivering an olive branch. That sounds like a terrific children's story, right? What they're also taught, however, is that a loving god they're supposed to worship was upset at the humans he created and loved, and killed everyone and everything on the planet except sea creatures, one man's family, and a sampling of animals. In this and other stories, impressionable children are taught that the god who loves them has no problem killing those who do not obey or pay enough attention to him. To a child, this can be very frightening, and in some cases, traumatizing.

Children are also taught in the story of David and Goliath that it's acceptable to wage war on and kill those who worship gods that are not the same as yours. And they're taught by Adam and Eve that a mistake their earliest ancestors made is a black mark on their souls unless they are baptized and saved from eternal damnation.

These examples only scratch the surface of childhood indoctrination. In many churches, kids are taught at an early age to recruit members by threatening their friends with stories of hell, preach to congregations in their churches by reciting back what has been burned into their memories as words you're supposed to say in the pulpit (but passed off as divinely-inspired wisdom that a child couldn't possibly fully understand), or stand along busy highways holding up signs warning others of their impending eternal doom unless they repent.

Again, these children did not embrace their religious convictions on their own. They did not wonder about the origins of the world and go on a journey of fact-finding and enlightenment. They were instructed what their beliefs should be based on the beliefs of their families, local communities, and expectations of others. They were not given an opportunity to vet the concepts taught to them by the people they trust the most. They lack the education and understanding of the world around them to be able to challenge doctrine taught by their churches. And they're taught to never question, as questioning their faith is a sin or a thought passed into their brains by the devil himself. Questioning the existence or the perfection of their god would anger this entity so much that they may be cast into a pit of flames forever. Don't do it.

Being raised in a Catholic family, I was one of those kids. Although my indoctrination and upbringing were not as extreme as some of the examples I mentioned, I was nonetheless told what my belief system would be comprised of, and was taught not to question. I was baptized into the Church as an infant and attended Catholic school from kindergarten to the end of 8th grade. During this time, I was guided through the required sacraments and milestones of Catholicism: First Confession and Penance, First Communion, and Confirmation. During these years, I attended religion classes in school, learning mostly about the Catholic Church and its history. We were spared the details about widespread slaughter of non-Catholics during the Crusades[2] and Spanish Inquisition.[3] The political details[4] surrounding the formation of the New Testament gospels were also skipped over, protecting our minds from anything that would reflect poorly on the Church. We weren't told the true history of the New Testament and it's formation by Emperor Constantine as a tool to control the people by replacing any non-Christian dogma with a new state religion, making Christianity law. Instead, the gory details accompanying the spread of Christianity

---

[2] Atrocities: The 100 Deadliest Episodes in Human History, Matthew White, W. W. Norton & Company, 2011

[3] The Spanish Inquisition: A History, Joseph Perez, Yale University Press, 2006

[4] http://www.livescience.com/2410-council-nicea-changed-world.html

throughout the world were presented in a positive way, and the leaders of the movement were heralded as heroes for Jesus. There was a lot of this type of spinning of historical truth in order to improve the image of early Christians, and it was quite irresponsible in my opinion. But in a Catholic school, the indoctrination of youth is top priority. I could go on about the injustices doled out during the Middle Ages, but the sordid history of the Church is not the focal point of this book.

The point is there was never a choice. As a child I, along with countless others, was not taught about the religions of the world in an impartial way. I was told what religion was the *right* one and that any others were total nonsense. For whatever reason, I remember a lesson in one of my religion textbooks where the religions of the world were listed out by popularity. We reviewed them in class, each student reading aloud about a different religion, briefly touching upon the main tenets of each faith system. I was comforted to learn that Christianity was at the top of the list, further showing me that we were right and everyone else was wrong. We laughed at some of the beliefs of other religions – some believed in reincarnation, or that Jesus wasn't divine, or that more than one god exists. I was also taught that atheism was an evil and ridiculous concept. No one questioned the teachers or the religious patriarch that surrounded us. We weren't allowed to. In fact, the Catholic religion was so ingrained in our everyday routine that there was never even a conscious thought to object.

And that's why childhood indoctrination is so effective. If religious leaders can sow their seeds into a developing mind at an early age, their rate of success is very high. If children are allowed to grow up without being religiously trained, they would much more readily reject religious tradition as young adults who no longer believe in magic and think more logically and rationally, rather than attributing all things unexplained to miracles or acts of a higher power. Imagine if you grew up with no religious instruction or contact, and only explained the natural world in scientific ways. You were taught about the origins of the universe, life, and human development through biology, anthropology, archeology, physics, and the other sciences. You weren't taught to attribute the unknown to a deity, but rather explained such topics as those we haven't discovered answers to yet. Then someone comes along and tells you that all of this came into being from a mystical deity and that this god sent his son in the form of a god-man combo who was killed in a symbolic effort to save everyone from the punishment his father was going to send them to. And in order to avoid this punishment, we need to have a personal relationship with this resurrected dead person that we can't see, hear, or have any evidence exists. Any rational adult who's hearing this for the first time would laugh at it and dismiss it just as we do with every other religion we weren't taught as kids to regard as the truth – Hinduism, Islam, Taoism, Greek and Roman gods, Buddhism – you name it. There are over 2,000 gods that have come and gone in the course of human history. Rational adults who hear outlandish claims like this for the first time, without any tangible evidence it's true, reject such claims. But children? Not necessarily. That's why these ideas need to be instilled as early as possible. Children don't seek religion. Adults seek it for them based on what *they* were taught as children.

In contrast, it can be said that a significant principle at the core of atheism is choice. The overwhelming majority of atheists have chosen to be nonbelievers. This path has been chosen not because it's a rebellious attitude or a trendy concept. In actuality, most atheists have reached their conclusions about religion based on evidence, or a lack thereof. Atheists tend to hold more esteem for logic and reason than for blind faith. No atheist will ever end an argument about the nonexistence of gods by saying, "well that's where faith comes in."

Although the atheistic outlook may not be favorable to the religious, it's still a valid world view, and those who adopt it are deserving of the same respect they had as believers, if not more, since this is a view that has been chosen based on critical thinking and a search for knowledge. On the other side of the coin, an argument can be made that most of the faithful have not chosen their path, but it has been provided for them by family tradition, time period of their life, and geography. For most subscribers of religion, we could assess that if they were born at a different time or on the other side of the planet, they would indeed hold a different religious conviction than they currently do. But can the same be said for the freethinking atheist? Would an atheist be an atheist regardless of these factors? It's a difficult question to answer, considering socioeconomic conditions and political pressures are different globally, and many are closely tied to religion. One factor remains though, that the level and type of education one has been exposed to (formal or informal) plays a huge contributing factor in the development of a person's religious affiliation.

Because of the opposition to childhood indoctrination's *modus operandi* of teaching young people what to think rather than how, believers will often notice a negative reaction from atheists to the heavy involvement of children in church activities like Sunday school, sacraments, evangelism and the like. While the reaction by the religious to this opposition may follow along the lines of defending indoctrination as teaching of morality or tradition, it's important for the believer to remember what drives the negativity. Atheists see indoctrination as a removal of choice, a blocking of free thought, and instilling the fear of eternal punishment for misbehaving or rejecting doctrine.

Because many nonbelievers have seen the effects of

indoctrination, most will raise their children not to be atheists, but to be rational thinkers who are encouraged to search for facts and make life decisions based on what they've uncovered. When the topic of religion comes up, many nonreligious parents will explain several religions to their children and present them as ideas that other people believe in. An atheist will not make those decisions for their children but instead will provide the means necessary for them to discover what they believe on their own. If a child decides to follow a particular religion, most nonbelieving parents will not stand in the way. Instead, they will support their children as they embark on the religious journey, encouraging them to think critically, seeking knowledge and truth along the way, rather than believing everything that they're told. Most atheists are more concerned with their children becoming good people and living their lives without harming others than what religion they subscribe to. The important theme is that each child is given the freedom to make religious choices when they're at a point in their intellectual development where they can comprehend complicated concepts like the origin of the universe or the possibility of an afterlife. The "4-14 window" should be a time filled with unbiased education, independent discovery, and above all, wonder – not indoctrination.

While the choice was made by my parents on my behalf, my wife and I haven't made that choice for our two children. Shortly after our first son was born in

2011, questions began coming in from family and close friends regarding when he would be baptized. As the majority of my wife's and my family is Catholic, that was the expectation. Most of the individuals posing these questions were not aware that we're both atheists, especially since we were married in a Catholic church. At the time of our wedding, my wife was still Catholic but struggling with her faith at times. We decided to get married in a church for more of a traditional purpose than a religious one. To be honest, during the religious portions of the ceremony, I tuned out, daydreaming about the Caribbean vacation we would spend the next week enjoying. When we're in uncomfortable situations, we do what we can to cope.

When asked about our son's baptism, I responded that we wouldn't be doing that, and most of the conversations ended there, usually with a surprised look or eye roll since this was a huge deviation from family tradition. For some, the discussion continued. There would be no godparents, no baptism celebration and gifts, and no wearing of the baptismal gown worn by the other members of the family who came before him. This was very upsetting to some, especially those closest to us. I fielded questions and statements like,

> "Why would you make him an atheist? Don't you want to give him a choice?"

> "Why don't you baptize him just in case he decides to be Catholic later?"

"You should do it for your family anyway. It doesn't mean anything to you."

"At least do it for the gifts."

Yeah, the last one gave me a chuckle. Going through this process was very eye opening for me and my wife. Although I expected people to ask about the potential baptism, I was not prepared for the negative reactions from family members who openly showed their disapproval of our parenting decision. What I realized though, is that they asked these questions because they didn't understand our point of view. This would prove to be an "aha" moment that ultimately paved the way for this book.

I attempted to explain to my family that baptizing my son was actually the opposite of giving him a choice. Initiating my infant son into a religious tradition was not a decision I wanted to make for him. Should he decide at some point that he would like to be religious, and his subscribed doctrine required him to pour water over his head as a symbolic cleansing of a sin he didn't physically commit, he would be free to do so.

At one point some conversations surfaced (whether in jest or not, we're not sure) around my son's grandparents contemplating getting him baptized without our knowledge. This was very troubling to us, since it would obviously be an outright betrayal of our trust and display of disrespect to us as parents. To my knowledge, no real attempt was ever made but the suggestion of such an action solidified the realization that healthy discussions between believers and nonbelievers need to happen more often so that conflicts like this can be avoided. If it happened to us, then I was sure it happened to other atheist parents as well.

In respect to religious tradition, nonreligious parents will often make parenting decisions that will be difficult to understand or will challenge these traditions. Like any other parents, nonbelievers make decisions that effect their children with their kids' best interests in mind. While religious family members may object to these decisions on a spiritual level, it's important to find out why the decision was made before saying or doing something to undermine the parents' wishes for their children.

If you have questions, it's ok to ask them in a tactful and nonthreatening way. I have yet to meet an atheist who is averse to discussing his or her thoughts about religion. As long as both parties have the child's welfare at heart, a constructive conversation can materialize. Keep in mind that a parent's decision can and should trump all. Making an effort to understand those decisions, rather than complain about or undermine them, will go a long way toward maintaining a positive and healthy family relationship.

3

THE JOURNEY

"We are all atheists about most of the gods that humanity has ever believed in. Some of us just go one god further."

-Richard Dawkins

KEVIN DAVIS

The journey from religion to freethought for each nonbeliever is different from the next. Some are raised without religion ever being a significant part of their lives, while the overwhelming majority were believers at some point in their lives and have abandoned theism for atheism. The former is fairly rare, especially in the United States, but is on the upswing, coinciding with the growth of the nonreligious demographic and the increasing popularity of secular parenting. As the community of the religiously unaffiliated grows in number, the frequency of childhood indoctrination declines, ultimately giving more children the freedom to choose their religious path. The latter – the religious-turned-atheist – generally goes through a process of awakening, made up of stages including a search for knowledge, rejection of prior education, "coming out," and realization that they're not alone. In order to truly understand the "de-converted" atheist, you must first understand that becoming an atheist is not a decision that is made on a whim. It's a thoughtful, and in many ways frightening, process based on education, thinking for oneself, overcoming of stigma and taboo, and coming to terms with mortality while rejecting the concept of eternal life.

After leaving parochial school at the conclusion of my 8th grade year, I was a typical American Catholic. Religion didn't play a major role in my life but I generally identified with the tenets of Catholicism. I attended church services on the occasional Sunday, but for the most part only went for weddings, funerals, and special services like baptisms and holidays. Since at this point in my life I hadn't mentally bought into religion hook, line, and sinker, it was more important to me to spend my Sundays with my friends playing sports outdoors or watching football. Beginning at age thirteen I attended public high school, and Catholicism was losing even more significance to me in a new secular environment. Ironically enough, in my high school years I would find myself surrounded by close friends who were very religious. This affiliation would soon play a large role in gaining an informal education about other Christian denominations outside the Catholic bubble I was raised in.

My best friend throughout high school was raised Christian and his father was the pastor at a small local church. His family was obviously very involved in the church, something that was foreign to me, but they never pushed their faith on me, even though their oldest son and I were basically inseparable. They still are some of the kindest people I've ever met, accepting me for who I was, and not taking advantage of the countless hours we spent together to try to "save" me or evangelize at every opportunity. I was occasionally invited to functions at their church, but my absence from those events was never an issue. My experience with his family is something that stays in the back of my mind whenever I find myself unfairly generalizing about all religious people. They taught me that believers can be welcoming, inclusive, and unprejudiced. While it's easy for atheists to paint a broad picture of the religious as closed-minded people following a literal interpretation of a two-thousand year old book of magic written before the age of modern science, positive past relationships with Christians like my friend's family help to keep me thinking more objectively.

My girlfriend's family was a bit of a different story though. Her father was also a pastor, but right away I felt the tension between me and her parents. They were Pentecostal, a segment of the Christian faith chock full of dramatic witnessing, speaking in tongues, driving away demons, and one hundred percent dedication to Jesus Christ. Upon meeting her parents, right off the bat I was asked about my religious affiliation, and since it was much different than theirs, the first thing I felt was judged. My girlfriend didn't push the issue too hard, but it was always an underlying point of contention that attached itself to our relationship through two high school proms and the beginning of my first year of college. She was my first love, and I was committed to overcoming this enormous obstacle, as difficult as it seemed. So when the invitation was presented to join her at her Christian youth group meeting, I obliged.

Compared to any religious gathering I'd ever attended, Christian youth group was exceptionally foreign. I was out of my league and I knew it from the start. Christianity was on display via uplifting songs played by a Christian rock band (rather than the organ and soloist I was used to in a Catholic church), Bible discussion, and testimony of youth group members who have witnessed the power of Christ in their lives. Many of the attendees had their hands raised in the air and were so deeply affected by the experience that they seemed nearly entranced by it. I had never seen anything like it. Although I'm sure it was normal to those who had been exposed to this level of religious concentration throughout their lives, it just wasn't common for Catholics in my life to talk about how much they loved Jesus and how awesome his effect was in their lives.

I was a sit-stand-kneel-chant Catholic, not a singing, dancing, hands in the air witness to Christ.

Despite my discomfort, I stayed until the end in my effort to appease and gain points with my girlfriend, but this would be my last youth group visit. I knew what the end goal was in this endeavor, and I wasn't ready to be "saved." These people were the real deal. This was not something I could fake. If we were to stay together, she would have to be ok with me being an acquaintance of Jesus rather than having a "personal relationship" with him.

Our relationship survived for a while after that, through the end of high school and into our first year of college – a state school for me and a private Christian college for her. But ultimately it was pressure from her parents that split us apart. The lack of acceptance I felt from them on day one carried on throughout our time together and she finally succumbed to their insistence, breaking it off after they had decided our relationship had gone on long enough. I was crushed, but there was always a part of me that thought it would eventually happen. We were too far apart on such an important piece of who she was that the rift would someday be too large to overcome. I suppose the breakup was the event that initiated my quest for some kind of religious closure. I had been emotionally affected by people who were so sure about their beliefs that they would make life altering decisions based on them, choosing spiritual love over earthly love.

Not too long after the breakup, I became aware that a couple of my new college friends were involved in a campus group known as the InterVarsity Christian Fellowship. They met once per week and I was invited to attend one evening, worked into our plans of party-hopping afterward. The invitation was presented as a no-pressure, be as active as you want, just check it out kind of thing. It seemed harmless enough so I tagged along. What I found was a college version of the church youth group I had attended with my girlfriend in high school. But since I was in a different place mentally, this time embarking on a search for religious answers, I decided to give it a chance and attend for at least a few weeks. In hindsight, I know now that I was the perfect candidate – someone going through a rough time in his life, on a search to find himself and discover what his own belief system should be. I was ready to be pointed in the direction toward Jesus. I was ready to be saved.

I continued to attend the IVCF meetings every week and made some friends within the group who would keep tabs on me and make sure I continued to attend. I started reading the Bible more frequently. I kept notes and asked my new friends questions about Christianity when I had them. I started going to church when I could. I met with my IVCF friends for private prayer sessions in dorm rooms. I was becoming a "born-again" Christian. Finally, I thought I had found what I was looking for. I would soon recite the Prayer of Salvation[5] and be considered "saved" by the group. I felt comfortable. I belonged.

Over the next break, I returned home and tested the

---

[5] http://www.salvationprayer.info/prayer.html

waters by evangelizing to my family, but in a way I thought was subtle, working faith into conversations when I could. I invited my parents to church with me in an effort to show them the Jesus Christ I now had a personal relationship with and how much different he was than the version we were presented with as Catholics. But as special occasion church attenders, they declined, most likely chalking up my new Bible-thumping personality as some kind of phase, so I attended by myself. While I was gaining confidence in my new Christian persona, I was still on a search for knowledge. But at this point, I focused that search on Christianity, the Bible, and any related topics I could find. I was no longer on an objective quest for truth. Instead, my new faith had redirected me to seek out knowledge supplied and endorsed by Christians. Somewhere along the line I picked up on the idea that secular information in regards to religion would lead me astray. I did my best to avoid it.

In the following semester, I registered for a course I felt would supply more of the theological insight I was seeking. It was called Christian Thought. Despite the philosophical-sounding title, this was a history course taught by a Christian and former politician that chronicled the origins of Christianity and its evolution into the religion that we know it to be today. Going into it, I thought the class would be a celebration of the Christian faith and would in turn strengthen and solidify my growing devotion to Christ.

This would prove to be a poor assumption.

Taking this course ended up being one of the most eye-opening experiences of my life. The class touched upon countless aspects of the history of the Christian faith that I never learned in my nine years of Catholic school education or in my current iteration of religious identity. Though much of what was touched upon was done so at a high level, it proved to be a launching point for my insatiable thirst for knowledge that would lead me to atheism in the end.

I would soon learn of the existence of gospels that were not included in the Bible[6], what they said about Jesus and his claims of divinity, and the political circumstances surrounding their exclusion from the New Testament. I learned that holidays we celebrated like Christmas and Easter began as pagan or secular holidays that were adopted by Christians and given religious significance. We also covered how tenets of the Christian faith such as the virgin birth, crucifixion, and resurrection were not unique to Jesus at all. They had all been referenced in some form or another by religions that had come and gone before Christianity. The basic foundations of the story of Jesus were all present in other, older religions. It seemed that Christianity was just a hybrid of several religions that came before it, recycled into a new narrative. I also

---

[6] Lost Scriptures : Books that Did Not Make It into the New Testament, Bart D. Ehrman, Oxford University Press, 2003

learned more about how Christianity was spread throughout Europe and the Americas, through war and mass murder. This course was obviously not what I expected it to be. I can imagine the other IVCF members who attended the same class had a similar reaction. Or it's possible they didn't, depending on what degree of critical thinking they applied to the concepts being addressed in the curriculum. Were they also surprised by what they were learning, or did they look past it all as a means to an end, feeling that the spread of Christianity was the greater good? I'll never know for sure, but for me, the destruction left in the wake of the spread of Christianity was something that deeply disturbed me and activated a sense of empathy that halted me in my tracks.

Was this something I wanted to be part of? Was I really being told "the Truth" and shown "the Way"? Why were such items of historical and religious significance kept from me for so many years?

At this point I began a renewed search for truth. I looked even further into the concepts I was learning in my Christian Thought course. I wanted to know more about the origins of the Christian faith. I blocked out all outside influence when it came to religion. I was back on the objective path. I wanted to find out for myself. If my fact-finding led me back to religion, then so be it, but from now on my attitudes on faith would be based on my own experiences and the evidence I discovered on my own.

I conducted my own theological research sporadically for a period of a few years before finally coming to terms with my own independent conclusion – it's all bullshit.

I came to the realization that gods were created by man to ease minds and give explanation and purpose to the otherwise unknown or unexplained. Further, religion was created by man to control populations and prevent chaos.

4

COMING OUT

"We can judge our progress by the courage of our questions and the depth of our answers, our willingness to embrace what is true rather than what feels good."

-Carl Sagan

Once an atheist rejects the dogma he's been taught and no longer believes in any gods, the road ahead is often a bumpy one. Becoming an atheist is not as simple as no longer attending religious services or celebrating holy days. Coming to terms with one's own lack of belief is a process that can elicit various emotions that, for some people, mirror the five stages of grief: denial, anger, bargaining, depression, and acceptance.

It's essential to remember that most atheists don't make a conscious decision to be an atheist. Again, it's a conclusion that someone has come to after weighing factors important to him or her, whether they be scientific findings, faulty holy books and dogma, religiously-based injustices, personal experiences, or a combination or reasons. So if the new nonbeliever was raised in a religious environment, the adjustment to this new outlook can be challenging, especially in terms of dealing with mortality. In the majority of religions, death and what happens after it are focused upon greatly. Specifically, believers are taught that living a righteous life or proper worship of a deity will pay off in an afterlife. The religious don't look at death as the end of all life. Instead, they look at death as the end of a life *on earth*, and the beginning of the immortal portion of their existence, be it in heaven, hell, or some other related spiritual realm. Religious dogma asserts solutions to the unknown and attributes its explanation to a divine being having the answer or being the answer. Since no one has died and come back to tell about it (debunked near-death experience phenomena aside), death becomes another unknown that fits well into the promotion of religious doctrine to fill in the blanks.

For the atheist though, death is the end. Most atheists believe that a human's life and death are no different than any other animal's. When humans die, their lives are over. There is no spiritual embarkation. There is no heaven or hell. This concept is so dramatically different than anything we're ever taught as believers that it can be difficult to grasp for both new atheists and their religious family and friends. Along with the removal of an afterlife from someone's belief system comes a departure from the comforting concepts that accompany dealing with death and mourning. Common words of solace like, "He's in a better place now," or "She's with her family again," no longer apply. An atheist will need to find a new way to deal with the death of loved ones. But more importantly, the new atheist will need to come to terms with his own mortality.

It's a scary thought – this is the only life you have, and as each day goes by, it's coming closer to an end. It's intensely frightening and difficult to accept, actually making it easier to understand the origins of religious belief. If we convince ourselves that we're something greater than other species, we can overcome this fear by giving ourselves immortality.

The concept of finality, as opposed to everything we've been taught in the past, is a cause of depression in some atheists. It can make us feel like an insignificant speck of dust in the universe. But for others, it can actually be awe-inspiring, or generate incentive to create meaning in one's life or to make a difference in the world while alive. Instead of living a good life in order to earn entry into paradise, an atheist will be motivated to live a good life in order to make the world a better place when he's gone. Sure, it sounds clichéd, but it's true. Atheists are motivated to do good works for the betterment of mankind or nature in general. That's not to say that religious people aren't motivated by the same, but an atheist's motivation is the answer to the question that is asked incessantly by the religious: "If you don't believe in God, then what reason do you have to be a moral or good person?"

This is a question that is seen as ridiculous to most atheists, because morality and religion are not mutually inclusive. It's not because of doctrine that religious people aren't out murdering people (actually in some cases it's *because* of doctrine that they *are*), and not all criminals are atheists, and vice versa. Most people generally do good works and avoid the harm of others because they're inherently compassionate and empathetic, not because someone told them they'd go to hell if they went buck wild on the world. In fact, as many atheists are Humanists, the argument can be made that they are even more concerned with the just treatment of fellow humans than some religious people who are more selfishly concerned with their own posthumous fate and relationship with their chosen deity.

Once an atheist works his way to his own internal "acceptance" phase, it's time to consider making his nonbelief known to his friends and family. Depending on the atheist's family situation and the level of religiosity of his community and loved ones, the coming out process can be a very different experience from person to person. There are some atheists I know who came out to their families and received a much more muted reaction than they were expecting, and some who came out to their loved ones and were shunned, thrown out of the house by parents, or totally cut off from their families. Depending on what religion is being rejected, the reaction of the new atheist's loved ones or community can be dictated by the church, such as the mandatory shunning we see from Jehovah's Witnesses.

But in more generally moderate traditions like Catholicism, Judaism, and some Christian denominations, the reactions of friends and family are often less severe but still very difficult to deal with. In my own experience in a Catholic family, my coming out was less of a singular event and more of a gradual removal from religious activities, leading up to a general understanding that I no longer believed in God. I was in my early 20s when my atheism came to be known, not too far removed from the time I was identifying myself as a "saved" Christian and a devout one at that. The initial reaction from my parents was that this was another phase I was going through in a search for my own religious identity, and rightfully so. After all, just a few years earlier I had been asking my parents to come to church with me and inserting my Christian faith into the conversation whenever possible.

But based on my own research, education, and application of critical thinking, my atheism was backed by scientific evidence, biblical shortcomings, and a focus on humanity rather than the supernatural. It was not a temporary phase and remains steadfast nearly 20 years later.

Since my identity as an atheist was not taken very seriously at the beginning, my coming out lacked the dramatic reaction that many others experience. Instead, I was met with some subtle and some not-so-subtle passive aggressive comments, eye rolls, jokes, and sarcastic digs throughout the years. While the intentions of many were merely on a harmless level, it was the constant insertion of religious nonbelief into otherwise innocuous conversations that proved to me that my atheism was at the forefront of the minds of my loved ones and began to define who I was in their eyes. I was no longer just the family member who loved watching and playing sports, traveling, and being with friends and relatives. I was still all of those things followed by "who is an atheist." I was different, even though I was still the same person. I was the first out of the closet atheist that many of my family and friends had known, if not all of them. I became the subject of little pranks at the family dinner table or at larger gatherings, frequently hearing things like, "Kevin, say grace," reminding me that this was something that was on people's minds. It was almost as if they wanted to address it but didn't know how. Instead of outwardly telling me they disapproved or it made them uncomfortable or they didn't quite understand it, they poked fun at it. I suppose that fits into the realm of normal human behavior. We often mock what we don't understand.

If we're being completely honest, sure, there were times that I made fun of their beliefs too. I mean, a talking snake? That's just silly.

At first, these glancing blows would make me upset but I wouldn't let on. In time, I began to stick up for myself and called an end to it, provided I would also keep my opinions of their beliefs to myself. That's fair I suppose, but it didn't address the larger issue. We really needed to talk about the elephant in the room. Little by little, the subject would come up in conversation but I wasn't going to push it. At this point it was more important to me to feel accepted by my loved ones than to make them understand my world view. I thought dropping the little jokes and snickers would bring back the feeling of acceptance I once felt around them. I was wrong.

In hindsight, I think it would have been beneficial to purposefully sit down with members of my family and discuss the atheism issue. It would be a more difficult conversation for some than others I'm sure, but it would have given me an opportunity to understand where everyone stood as well as give me a forum to explain how I felt around them and that I was no different than the son, brother, or cousin they already loved and respected.

If people understood my position, the subtle jokes here and there would have lost their passive aggressive undertones and changed their meanings. The teases would be more tolerable and be just that – sarcastic digs that are already part of my family dynamic. But hindsight is 20/20.

Over the years, my religious beliefs, or lack thereof, would occasionally be brought up in conversation, but to my delight, not usually in a way that would cause harm. I found that as my family and friends became more comfortable with my views, the questions started coming in slowly:

"What do you think happens when you die?"

"Do you believe in a soul or spirit?"

"Why don't you go to church just in case you're wrong?"

I was surprised to hear questions like these get asked, but was delighted at the same time. People closest to me were starting to make an effort to understand my viewpoint. I was sure to address each and every question, and even though I knew those close to me would disagree with me in the end, I was happy to help them understand that I didn't come to these conclusions on a whim. My atheism was a conclusion I reached based on thoughtful consideration of everything around me. Once I had an opportunity to explain that, I could see, feel, and hear a growing respect for who I presented myself to be – a well-informed critical thinker who came to his own conclusions by rejecting the influence of others.

As a result of these somewhat random one-off conversations, what I found in some of my friends and family was honesty. People began to open up to me about their own skepticism, or even religious devotion.

They found themselves comfortable enough to share what was on their minds about their own faith, whether it be the way they disagree with some of the teachings of their own religion, or what times in their lives they feel they had a "religious experience" that helped to reinforce their faith. As these exchanges happened, I knew that these were rare conversations. It wasn't common to discuss religious beliefs in my family or group of friends. It was just understood that you believed. Most of us were raised Catholic and went to church when it was required, no questions asked.

The newfound honesty I was surrounded by was a surprise to me. I hadn't expected it, but in the end, regardless of what we did or did not agree on, the conversations alone immediately strengthened relationships. Those around me were more comfortable and at ease, especially when anything about religion would come up. The elephant was fading and we could be honest with each other.

My only regret is that these conversations took over ten years to commence. Up until then, the elephant was alive and well, waving at me from the end of the dinner table as soon as the blessing began.

5

IN THE OPEN

"I know I was born and I know that I'll die.
The in-between is mine. I am mine."
-Eddie Vedder/Pearl Jam
I Am Mine

Revealing one's atheism to the outside world can happen prior to coming out to family or afterward, depending on how close knit the family is, whether the individual lives in the same city, state, or country as his relatives, or depending on that person's comfort level with his own disbelief.

Letting the rest of the world know about your true identity, thoughts, feelings, and beliefs is much easier now than it has ever been with the availability of social media outlets and topical blogs. Facebook, Twitter, Reddit and others have become places for people of all faiths to meet and share ideas regardless of geography. Social media websites have become safe havens for those looking to venture outside of their physical surroundings and learn more about people they wouldn't normally come into contact with. Finding a venue to connect with other atheists is an important step toward gaining the confidence needed to come out of the atheism closet and become comfortable with this new ideological identity.

A new nonbeliever will have questions. Remember, this is usually someone who, for his or her entire life has been taught the complete opposite of what is now believed to be true by that person. Today more than ever, answers to those questions are available within seconds via online support groups, blogs, videos, podcasts, and a myriad of books and articles written by popular secular authors like Richard Dawkins, Sam Harris, Christopher Hitchens, and Daniel Dennett.

As new nonbelievers seek out answers to the questions they have, it is inevitable that they will come across the religion-based social and political issues facing the secular world, such as LGBTQ rights, science education, indoctrination of children, political influence of religious institutions, and separation of church and state. They will likely discover injustice and discrimination against atheists, and many will make a decision to learn more, ultimately becoming involved. As a friend or family member of a new atheist, you may notice him or her posting on social media about court cases involving religious discrimination or other secular hot button issues. You may overhear conversations about political issues, books being read, or even conventions attended.

It's important to remember that the recently reclassified nonbeliever is venturing on a path that is fresh and new to him. It's exciting for him to share his new knowledge and understanding with others, just as it is exciting for a religious person to share Bible verses, or even schoolchildren to demonstrate their new knowledge to their parents. Even though you may disagree with the message, this time of discovery and openness shouldn't be treated with shunning or disdain. Your loved one is sharing this information with you, most likely not to "de-convert" you, but because you are a person he loves, respects, and wants to have a conversation with. It's ok to change the subject sometimes if it becomes an annoyance, just as long as you're not shutting the door to conversation completely. An overwhelmingly negative reaction to the discussion could be perceived as a disinterest in *any* conversation because you disagree with the person's new world view.

In time, the new nonbeliever will have tested the waters with many loved ones to see who it's safe to have religious or political conversations with, and who closes that door altogether. Those who close the door may be sending a message of general non-acceptance. While those people may disagree with their loved one's views on atheism, secularism or related issues, those views must be held separate from their feelings toward the person holding the views. Changing the subject of the conversation sends a much different message to the new atheist than avoiding all contact or discussion completely. If the subject matter of a religious conversation causes uneasiness or discomfort, it's perfectly acceptable and respectful to say something like, "I'd like to talk about something else. I respect you and your passion, but I'd rather talk about this topic some other time."

Atheism does not define a person, just as Christianity, Islam, or Judaism doesn't. So it's important to convey that your feelings for your atheist loved one have not changed. You may disagree on the topic of religious belief or origin of the universe, but in the end, your friend or family member is still the same person you love, trust, and respect. Atheism is a lack of belief. So just like anyone else, atheists are not defined by who they're *not*. They are defined by who they *are* – the same person they were, but without religion.

If in fact you're comfortable discussing topics important to the nonbeliever in your life, you will likely notice you've achieved a new level of respect with your freethinking friend. In the process, you'll probably learn a bit about social and political issues that you normally wouldn't be exposed to. In the current U.S. political climate, the Religious Right is becoming more influential in public policy and election strategy. Since they are more active in the conservative Republican movement, it's very likely that the atheist in your life will become left, liberal, or progressive-leaning. You may also find that the atheist and LGBTQ movements are closely linked, since both groups are confronted with similar social, political, familial and religious shaming. Because of this treatment, it's very common for people who identify as LGBTQ to leave religion.

Becoming active in the atheist community is not a road that all atheists take, but it's becoming more and more common, especially in the United States. In a highly polarized society, many see a "war on religion" happening while others may perceive a "war on freedom" or "war on science" in progress. While none of these are physical conflicts, people on each side recognize them to be just as damaging, if not more so.

Once a budding atheist activist becomes more comfortable out in the open, he or she may choose to become involved with one or several secular organizations. Many of these organizations may be familiar to the religious majority by name, but not by mission, since they're often negatively represented in the media or within religious institutions. Unfortunately, the vast majority of times that atheist activist organizations are mentioned in the news it's due to a highly publicized lawsuit or protest. In order to promote a better understanding of who these groups are and what they are working toward, I've listed some of the larger ones here, in no particular order.

American Atheists *(atheists.org)* – An organization dedicated to a complete separation of church and state. The group is known to file suit against those who violate the First Amendment's Establishment Clause, which forbids religious favoritism by the government.

They also hold conventions, demonstrate in public protests, grant scholarships to young activists, and house the nation's largest atheist library. American Atheists' leaders make frequent media appearances to represent secular views in panel discussions or in interviews where the subject matter is relevant to their cause.

Center for Inquiry *(centerforinquiry.net)* – CFI's mission is to foster a secular community based on reason, science, freedom of inquiry, and humanist values. CFI is known for its work in education, advocacy, and outreach to other organizations.

Secular Coalition for America *(secular.org)* – Located in Washington, D.C., SCA lobbies the U.S. Congress, White House, and federal agencies on issues facing the secular community. SCA provides a much-needed voice for secular Americans on Capitol Hill.

Freedom From Religion Foundation *(ffrf.org)* – FFRF publishes Freethought Today, a secular newspaper, available to donors. The organization also hosts conventions and is well known for thought-provoking billboard campaigns and legal battles involving church-state separation issues.

Americans United for Separation of Church and State *(au.org)* – AU is an organization dedicated to church-state separation issues. Americans United does most of their work in federal and state legislatures and in the courts.

Secular Student Alliance *(secularstudents.org)* – SSA is a national organization connecting on-campus secular student groups through a national network to become more effective. SSA holds regional summits and an annual national conference focused on providing leadership training and networking assistance to students.

There are many other secular activist groups in the U.S. and around the world, ranging in purpose from political activity, to legal action, to support groups for people who have escaped traumatic religious oppression.

Becoming involved in secular advocacy or activist groups is important to many nonbelievers. Studies have consistently shown atheists to be among the least trusted and least liked demographics in the U.S. This is due to the broad misunderstanding of the group. The growing number of donors and activists involved with atheist organizations shows us a couple things. First, non-theists are becoming more comfortable with their identities and working to remove the stigma that accompanies "atheist" in American society. And second, these activists are seeing the need for equality and fighting back against those who claim the U.S. to be a Christian nation based on biblical foundations and laws, despite quotes from the Founding Fathers and the Supreme Court's interpretation of the First

Amendment explaining otherwise. To quote the Treaty of Tripoli, signed by John Adams and ratified by the Senate in 1797, "the Government of the United States of America is not, in any sense, founded on the Christian religion."

In my own search for political identity, I've come across the work of many of these groups through news reports, social media, and my own research. I've donated to some and become involved with others, including the now defunct political party, the Secular Party of America (previously known as the National Atheist Party). I was drawn to this group because its focus was to bring secularism deeper into the political arena with an ultimate goal of supporting candidates for political office. While we're all aware of the black eye of atheism in our culture, no more present is it than in politics. Some states even go so far as to have laws on the books preventing atheists from running for office. Nowhere else is the uphill battle of atheists greater than in government representation. As of the writing of this book, no out of the closet atheist serves in any of the three branches of our federal government (there has only been one in the nation's history). That's zero out of over 500 people, in a country made up of 10-15% nonreligious people. What this possibly means is that at least 50 elected federal-level politicians are lying about their religious affiliation in order to earn and keep their jobs.

The mission of the Secular Party was to have the

values of the nonreligious represented in government, most notably the complete separation of church and state. During my time with the party I held two positions, Social Media Director and Blog Editor. The party would fall apart though, not ironically, amid a scandal involving an internal voting fraud led by members of its Executive Board.[7] It was a controversy that rocked the organization so deeply that its members fled quickly, recognizing the damage that had been done and knowing that the dishonesty within the party would become synonymous with its atheist membership if the group would continue to operate. With a base demographic already deemed untrustworthy by the majority of Americans (according to multiple studies over the past 40 years),[8] the party no longer had any hope of political success once there was a black mark on its record.

At this point, my desire for activism was directed toward a local atheist "Meetup" group involved in community service projects and local activism, as well as several online groups aimed at discussing national secular issues. While still donating to a couple of the larger organizations, I was enjoying becoming more active at the local level while publishing blogs on my website at the time, *DividedUnderGod.com*.

---

[7]http://www.patheos.com/blogs/secularvoices/2013/09/09/secular-party-vote-fraud/
[8]http://atheism.about.com/od/atheistbigotryprejudice/a/AtheistSurveys.htm

The site was launched in 2011 after an eye-opening conversation I had on Facebook with a religious fundamentalist who happened to be a friend of a friend. The conversation began with a discussion about the Pledge of Allegiance and the insertion of "under God," added in 1954. A friend of mine had posted something about the topic. Being an atheist with strong feelings about the separation of church and state, I replied with reasons why the phrase should be removed from the pledge and why I felt it doesn't belong. The conversation was respectful until a friend of hers jumped in, adding her mistrust of evolution to the mix, claiming that it is "just a theory" and is therefore unproven. She followed up by quoting the Bible's story of creation, presenting it as fact. Being someone who always had an interest in science, particularly biology, I was well-aware of Darwinian evolutionary theory and other ideas that had been previously presented and debunked in an effort to explain the origin of man and other creatures on this planet. I also understand the difference between the layperson's definition of "theory" and the scientific definition that accompanies the Theory of Evolution by Natural Selection, a principle confirmed through experimentation and observation. The common use of *theory* and the definition of *scientific theory* are quite different. However, someone defending an anti-evolution stance will refer to evolution being a theory with the same validity as a hypothesis. Evolutionary theory is not a guess however. It's far from it, actually. It serves as a basic foundation of all modern biology.

Without an understanding of evolution, we would not have many of the medical advances we do today.

The conversation helped me realize that if this person was so adamant about the correctness of her unscientific viewpoint, then she must have learned it from somewhere. And if she was taught that the story of Genesis is true in a literal sense, then there are others who believe the same. I was inspired to launch a website that would bring to light the cases of judicial or legislative action meant to undermine the separation of church and state. I was, and still am, convinced that religious belief should be removed from school science programs and textbooks, because it's not science. It's the complete opposite. Religion has its place in religion classes or in churches, but not in a classroom filled with students who are being taught that science is based on verifiable facts.

On a broader scale, the articles on *DividedUnderGod.com* were focused on the removal of all religious bias or favoritism from government. Through the site, I was able to raise awareness to these issues and create a loyal following. Since then, the site has gone through a rebranding, I've brought on additional guest writers, and its popularity continues to grow under its current name, *SecularVoices*. The site is now hosted on the Patheos network, a popular conglomeration of columns from many different religions, including no religion. I'm grateful to those who read *SecularVoices* and share my posts on social media, using my articles as conversation starters.

6

WHAT IT MEANS

"Our belief is not a belief. Our principles are not a faith. We do not rely solely upon science and reason, because these are necessary rather than sufficient factors, but we distrust anything that contradicts science or outrages reason. We may differ on many things, but what we respect is free inquiry, open-mindedness, and the pursuit of ideas for their own sake."

-Christopher Hitchens

The preceding has been a glimpse into what an atheist experiences in his or her journey, popularly coined "from religion to reason." Once an atheist is out of the closet and living their life free from religion, their theist contacts will undoubtedly have questions that they're uncomfortable asking or are unsure how to go about asking.

In this chapter, I'll attempt to list and answer some of these questions (most of which are questions I've been personally asked by religious friends and family), not as a substitute for conversation between believers and nonbelievers, but to give the religious an idea of what types of responses to expect. Again, the responses listed undoubtedly will not represent all atheists. The most effective way to find out your loved one's views on these topics is to initiate the conversation.

Why do you hate God?

Another form of this question is, "Why are you angry at God?" The short answer is that an atheist doesn't hate God, and is not angry at God either. By definition, atheists cannot harbor any resentment toward any gods, because an atheist doesn't believe that any gods exist. In fact, it's more common for a Christian or other theist to go through a period of "hating God," because a theist believes God exists. Asking an atheist if she hates God is equivalent to asking her if she hates unicorns, sasquatches or dragons, since to her, they're all fictional figures. What would your response be if someone asked you why you hate unicorns?

The assumption of hating or being angry at God is a very common misconception among the religious. God-hating atheists are discussed in sermons, bible study, Sunday school, and many other religious forums. As explained earlier, the truth of the matter is that no atheist hates God. It's true that many nonbelievers hold hostility toward religion or the concept of gods in general. This is usually due to the harm that atheists perceive as being done in the name of religion. For example, childhood indoctrination, anti-science education, and religion-based public policy are just some areas that cause atheists to get hot under the collar. This can be misconstrued (and oversimplified) as hate for God, but in reality, it's contempt for the actions of the religious on behalf of (what atheists believe to be) an imaginary entity.

Why don't you go to church 'just in case'? or What if you're wrong?

This is also asked as, "Why don't you just believe in God in case you're wrong?" This is known as Pascal's Wager – the theory that it's safer to believe in God and be wrong than not believe and suffer his wrath if he does exist. It's a form of hedging your bet. If you believe and you're wrong, there is no punishment, but if you fail to believe and he exists, then he will be angry and you will be damned to hell. Pascal's wager is not logically sound. It assumes that the Christian God (or whatever deity the asker has subscribed to) is the only possible god, and thus you've successfully hedged your bet and can't lose. However, there have been thousands of gods throughout the history of man, so your odds of believing in the right one are already very slim – less than 1 in 2,000. It's much more important for an atheist, or any person for that matter, to be true to himself than to live a lie, feigning belief in something he doesn't truly believe in his heart.

If I'm asked this question, depending on who asked it, I'll occasionally respond by asking why the other person doesn't believe in Zeus "just in case." Sure, it's a snide answer, but when you're asked the same question a hundred times, sarcasm tends to creep in.

Most Christians aren't literalists when it comes to the Bible. Most have their own take on what's important in the book, usually based on the Golden Rule, living a fair and just life, or treating others in a loving way. So for some that are concerned about the fate of my soul, I offer this:

If there is a god, and it is a fair and just god, then I believe such a being will be more concerned about how well I've treated others than how often I went to church, prayed to it, or worshipped it. If I've lived a good life, inflicted little to no harm on others, demonstrated generosity, and showed love to the people I've come into contact with, then that should be good enough for such an entity. If it isn't, and the god demands that, on top of all the good I've done, I should have spent time bowing to it and praising it, then that god is truly a narcissist, and not benevolent as we're taught, and is therefore not a being that I would care to spend eternity with in the first place.

Is it ok to pray at meals when you're over for dinner?

Of course it is.

There's no reason for believers to set their own beliefs aside just because they're in mixed company. I attend family dinners at least a few times each month where the host or other guests lead a prayer before eating, often while holding hands around the table. I have no issue with this at all. I participate in the hand-holding as a gesture of harmony and stay silent during the prayer. Sure, it's not my favorite time of the day, but it does no harm to me to be present for a prayer. Besides, it would do much more harm to family relationships to excuse myself from the prayer, make an issue out of it, or to protest. No one is forcing me to worship and no one is persecuting me. I'm simply opting out but respecting others at the table by remaining silent.

The gesture is similar to a Jewish person attending a Christian wedding. While their views don't coincide, the Jewish attendee wouldn't normally protest the Gospel verses being read or stomp out of the church when the resurrection of Jesus is mentioned. That individual would take part in the ceremony when appropriate and opt out of receiving the Eucharist or reciting certain prayers with the congregation if he or she chose to.

Why do you still celebrate Christmas and other religious holidays?

Most, if not all, Christian holidays have roots or traditions that are secular or pagan. Even Pope Benedict XVI was quoted in agreement that Jesus could not have been born in December and that Christmas is symbolic of the birth of Christ, not necessarily a literal birthday celebration. Aside from that, many traditions that accompany Christmas have nonreligious roots tied to the winter solstice or the Roman Saturnalia, such as trees, gifts and mistletoe.

For most, the holidays have become more about celebrating family and relationships than religion. Most atheists celebrate Christmas and other holidays for the secular aspects: gift giving, feasting, and enjoying time with family. Holidays or holy days that are strictly religious, such as Good Friday, Palm Sunday or Ash Wednesday, are not typically celebrated by atheists.

If you don't believe in God, where does your moral compass come from?

The concept that morality comes from religion is simply false. As children, we begin to learn right from wrong from our parents or guardians. Religious doctrine isn't normally brought into the fold until we're old enough to understand it. Do Christian parents tell their toddlers not to hit other children because it's a sin? I think not. And is the Bible or Ten Commandments the only thing standing in the way of Christians from senselessly killing each other? I would hope not.

Our morals are derived partly from instinct and a natural sense of empathy, but mostly from learned behavior. Both religious and nonreligious people are moral because we've developed a compassion for fellow humans. Humans are social by nature, and displaying these moral traits is essential in maintaining a safe, fair, and harmonious society.

It's also important to understand that many, if not most, atheists are Humanists (also known as secular humanists). Secular humanists don't believe that humans are born inherently evil or tainted with sin, as is the case with many religious faiths. Humanists recognize the ethical consequences of decisions that people make rather than focusing on the spiritual consequence. These are consequences that affect humanity or nature, rather than a person's soul. In this world view, a person's reward or punishment for their actions is based on the effects they see or learn from those actions in the natural world rather than with a promise of paradise or torment.

Why do you seem so angry?

I suppose this is more of a personal question than one that applies to all of the nonreligious. However, many atheists do exhibit anger toward religion or the religious. This can be attributed to a few different sources. Many atheists are upset by what they perceive as the negative effects of religion. As discussed earlier, many atheists compare forms of childhood indoctrination to child abuse, a subject that could certainly get a rise out of a nonbeliever. Atheists may also show anger about injustices directed toward them as a member of the nonreligious. Because of the social aversion to atheists, it has become acceptable to speak out against them, generalizing about them as an evil or untrustworthy group. This type of treatment is not acceptable and considered hate speech if directed toward any other demographic. Most certainly, an angry or frustrated response to this outward disdain is understandable.

If you don't believe in God and heaven, how does your life have any meaning?

Atheists find meaning in their lives in the same way that believers do. We find joy in spending time with our families, friends, and loved ones. We celebrate accomplishments, plan for the futures of ourselves and children, and take pride in our work and successes.

Some would even argue that not believing in an afterlife brings more meaning and happiness to one's life than living life in expectation of an eternal reward. Let me explain:

All atheists come to the realization or conclusion that an afterlife is something that is fictional and used by religions to motivate their followers, but also to frighten and control them at times. For many, the lack of an afterlife is a difficult concept to accept, especially considering some atheists' level of prior indoctrination. Being atheists forces us to accept our own mortality. However, accepting our own mortality can help to find joy and meaning in the life we are living now. Atheists live in the present, rather than living for the promise of better things to come. We focus on enjoying the time we have with family and friends. We treat people with kindness, compassion, and respect because it's the right and humane thing to do, not because it will earn us an eternal reward. We don't waste our time on Earth in a selfish quest to gain the approval of a god that no one can prove the existence of. Instead, we spend our short time here doing what we can to make it better for the people we love and earn our places in their hearts and memories.

What do you think happens when you die?

You die.

Atheists believe that human death is no different than the death of any other animal. Our bodies decompose and become part of the earth (if we allow them to), just as every other living organism. Related questions are often focused around so-called near-death experiences, where a person's heart stops and they see a bright light or family members who have already passed away. Since there are scientific explanations for these experiences, I won't get into them too deeply, except to say that a nonbeliever attributes this phenomenon to neurological activity rather than something supernatural. There are numerous resources available that explain near-death experiences much better than I could, so I won't pretend to be a neuroscientist.

Doesn't it take even more faith to be an atheist?

I've been asked this question a few times and it still baffles me. The very definition of faith is the belief in something despite a lack of evidence for its truth, or a preponderance of evidence against it. Religious believers have faith because they don't have physical proof. Atheists don't need faith, because their lack of belief is founded on, or is a result of, a lack of evidence. Sure, it's impossible to prove that a god does not exist. It's also impossible to prove that unicorns don't exist. But it does not take faith to believe they don't. That belief is built on a lack of evidence, and is a reasonable conclusion based on having no proof to the contrary.

On the other side, religious people base their entire belief system on faith. Not only do they believe in a supernatural being despite the lack of evidence to support such a claim, but they also exercise faith in believing that the god they suggest exists is the correct one out of the thousands that have been presented as truth throughout human history.

Isn't atheism just another religion? I heard there are even atheist churches now.

Most atheists will argue that atheism is not a religion. It's simply a term used to identify the lack of belief in a god. A popular response to this question is, "Atheism is a religion in the same way 'off' is a television channel." Atheism does not come with a set of rules to live by, tenets to believe, or doctrine to practice. Atheists come from a wide range of backgrounds and believe different things. They embrace varied versions of morality, justice, and worldviews. Again, atheism defines who someone is *not*, rather than who someone is. While some generalizations can be made about atheists (such is the topic of this book, after all), these are merely high-level observations and not rules to live by as you'd find with a religion.

Atheist churches, also known as Sunday Assembly, have been on the rise in Europe and North America. They basically serve as a godless replacement for the camaraderie and community that comes with belonging to a church. They tend to be a celebration of secularism rather than a repeated ritual dedicated to an omnipotent overseer. And they're not for everyone. Many atheists are very much opposed to the existence of atheist churches, since they give that perplexing impression of atheism being a religion. The existence of such organizations is confusing to many, and because of this, I'm not a huge fan of them.

7

CHANGING PERCEPTIONS

"Christians talk as though goodness was their idea but good behavior doesn't have any religious origin. Our prisons are filled with the devout."

-Andy Rooney

When atheists or atheism is mentioned in the press, by religious leaders, or by politicians, it's almost always identified with negativity or controversy. Atheists and their associated advocacy groups gain headlines with lawsuits, protests, conventions and billboard campaigns. Rarely are nonbelievers portrayed as having a positive impact in the world. It's not surprising that with the rise of sensationalism in the news, atheist groups who succeed with a constructive influence are overlooked outside of the atheist community.

While many atheists hold anti-theist views (meaning they hold contempt for religion and in most cases would like to see it eradicated), the majority of atheists also hold humanistic views, valuing the human race as individuals and collectively. Because of this, several organizations of nonbelievers have been created and are active in benevolent work with no ties to religion. This approach to helping the fellow man is a "no strings attached" methodology, meaning there is charitable work being done by atheists with no introduction to a deity, no spiritual counseling, and no persuasive dogmatic literature being distributed. Secular organizations are becoming more active in the world and are doing so without an agenda.

Groups like these are actively attempting to change the negative perception that plagues atheists every day. Along with these organizations, individual atheists are working toward promoting a positive view of the nonreligious. Through podcasts, blogs, social media and open dialogue, many atheists are discarding old anti-theistic discourse for a more progressive approach.

Realizing that an adversarial relationship with the religious may be detrimental to the effort to change perceptions of atheists, some are beginning to embrace those believers who have more liberal or progressive views when it comes to doctrine. These atheists would rather be looked upon as Humanists who advocate for the equal treatment of all people, regardless of faith. As we are all members of the human race, it's important to work together for the betterment of humanity and the rest of the planet.

In terms of doing good works, disagreeing with someone's worldview or the tenets of a person's religion should not preclude you from working with that person for the betterment of humanity. It will be the ability to set aside those differences that will determine the success of all of us.

This shift in attitude is something I call *progressive atheism*. Since atheists argue that their nonbelief does not define them as human beings, neither should a person's particular religion. People should not be prejudged, rejected, or hated solely based on what belief system they subscribe to, but should be judged on their own words and actions instead. If those actions warrant criticism, then the focus should be placed there rather than on the potential for bad deeds based on dogma or a preconceived generalization.

Take this Pew Research study published in 2014, for example. When Americans were asked how they would feel about a family member marrying an atheist, here's how they responded (broken down by political tendencies):

How would you react if an immediate family member were to marry ...

Someone who doesn't believe in God

	Unhappy	Doesn't matter	Happy
Total	49	47	4
Consistently cons	73	24	2
Mostly conserv	58	39	3
Mixed	51	46	3
Mostly liberal	41	54	5
Consistently liberal	24	66	10

Source: 2014 Political Polarization in the American Public
Notes: Ideological consistency based on a scale of 10 political values questions
"Doesn't matter" includes "don't know"
responses. Percentages many not add to 100% because of rounding

PEW RESEARCH CENTER

This graphic highlights the prejudice encountered by atheists every day. It's an uncanny prejudice at that, in that it's accepted or even encouraged by many religious people who share a disdain for atheists. Could you imagine if this poll was about a race of people or disability, or even about the religious? The outrage by the "persecuted" would be remarkable.

Progressive atheism requires a paradigm shift from anti-theism to acceptance. Rather than focusing on debating the religious or pointing out the flaws of religious thought, progressive atheists are concerned with promoting a positive image of atheism through good works, open dialogue with the religious, and advocating for harmony.

Identifying as a progressive atheist does not coincide with an abandonment of the secular movement, however. In many cases, it's quite the opposite. A progressive atheist is still concerned with the political, legal and equal rights efforts mentioned earlier, but with the added dimension of reaching out to sympathetic progressive faith groups to work together when possible. And a progressive atheist may still find it important to debate the religious privately or publicly and even hold anti-theistic views. Many times atheists debate the religious publicly, not to try to sway the opinion of their opponents, but to show other closeted atheists that it's okay to come out and be heard. They are not alone.

In it's simplest form, progressive atheism is about promoting a positive image of atheism and setting differences aside when necessary to work toward a common goal.

For a new nonbeliever, progressive atheism isn't something that is normally adopted right away. As mentioned earlier, a recently de-converted person will experience emotional stages similar to the stages of grief. During the anger stage, a new nonbeliever may be in a state of mind where he wants nothing to do with religious individuals and would like nothing more than to expose the delusion of religion at every turn. This is when anti-theism and outward attacks on religion are most common. But a progressive atheist eventually moves past that and shifts his focus to promoting a positive image that will fight back against the stigma attached to the word "atheist."

8

MOVING FORWARD

"People who are atheists, they hate God, they hate the expression of God, and they are angry with the world, angry with themselves, angry with society and they take it out on innocent people who are worshipping God."

-Pat Robertson

As modern society evolves and taboos are replaced by acceptance of diversity, atheists will eventually be a welcomed and understood segment of our culture, just as they are throughout much of the rest of the world. We can point to ethnic groups and other demographics throughout history that had been previously distrusted or not well liked but are now embraced as part of the fabric of our nation, including the Irish, Italians, Jews, Catholics, homosexuals, and many more. There will be a day that atheists are considered as mainstream as these other groups, but it will take work.

Secular advocacy groups take legal action against those who discriminate against the nonreligious, in an effort to uphold our constitutional rights. Individual atheists are no longer accepting their role as an unspoken minority and are standing up for themselves in the face of the religious majority. Many more atheists are speaking out in blogs, podcasts, documentaries and books in order to raise awareness and let others who are closeted nonbelievers know that it's ok to come out and be open about who they are.

And as a result, those who used to have a preprogrammed notion about atheists are beginning to allow their views to change. Believers are beginning to accept those who may not subscribe to faith. Atheists are beginning to be judged by theists on their own merits as humans, not based on the dogma instilled in believers by religious leaders who taught that atheists were evil, lost, or unapproachable.

Even though perceptions of atheists may be slowly shifting, there is still an uphill climb to get where we need to be. The ultra-religious are fighting the progress of the atheist movement at every turn, accusing us of trying to destroy Christmas and other holidays, trying to destroy democracy, or even attempting to destroy America as we know it. These battles are often materialized as vicious political attacks, and the basis of these claims against atheists are either unfounded, twisted to fit a specific narrative, or altogether misunderstood.

What most atheists in the movement want is to be treated as fairly as the religious under the law. We want to have the right to be free from religion and not confronted with it everywhere we look. We want to keep religious doctrine from being taught as fact in public school classrooms. Religious dogma should be taught in churches, not science class. We want religion removed from politics and legislative influence. Laws should be based on the common good, public safety, and protection of life, liberty, and the pursuit of happiness. They must not be based on conformity to any specific faith.

While the nonreligious fight for these freedoms and the enforcement of constitutional rights, they will continue to be vilified by the religious majority, in a strategic move to maintain control.

So to the believers reading this book in order to gain a more thorough understanding of your atheist loved ones, I present this challenge:

Shield yourselves from the negativity directed toward atheists by those who criticize and generalize – religious leaders, politicians, media outlets and anyone else with an agenda. Trust that your nonreligious friend or relative is the same person he was before you knew he was not a believer. Show him love, compassion, and an open heart. Talk to him. Ask him if his thoughts and experiences align with what you've learned in these chapters. Begin the discussion in an effort to better understand your atheist loved one. You may be surprised by what you discover.

You don't have to agree to show you care, and you don't have to preach to show love. Opening the door to a discussion about who we are can strengthen relationships, create a mutual understanding, and bridge the gap caused by a difference in ideologies.

The first step in removing taboo is to kill the elephant.

9

EXPERIENCES SHARED

"We must question the story logic of having an all-knowing all-powerful God, who creates faulty humans, and then blames them for his own mistakes."
-Gene Roddenberry

My guess is that you made it through this book because you sincerely desire to understand what makes your nonbelieving loved ones tick so that you can improve your relationship with them. I applaud the effort you're making and assure you that you're far from alone.

During the process of writing this, I came into contact with a handful of religious people who may have had a similar experience to the one you're having now. They've shared their personal experiences with me and have allowed me to share them with you so that this divide can cease to exist, or at least become narrower.

In the following submissions written by believers, you'll encounter individuals who have been confronted with the dilemma of having atheist family members and have struggled with how to approach the elephant in the room. These examples are included, both to reassure you that it can be done, and to provide you with some examples of how the topic can be approached and the impasse overcome.

Julie S.
Phoenix, Arizona

My twin sister, Brenda, and I grew up in a devoutly Christian household. We were the only two children our parents had, and we are part of a very tight-knit family. As identical twins, it's safe to say we had an identical childhood. We did everything together, including attending church and youth group since before I can remember.

Somewhere along the line, Brenda lost her faith. She said it was a gradual process and began in high school. Looking back, I can see it now since she was always more interested in science, while I spent my time involved with the arts – music and theater. At 34, she finally told me she didn't believe in God, and I was the first she told. She never told our parents and they had passed away prior. She was too afraid of the reaction she thought they'd have. She knew what our mom and dad thought about atheists, because we all had attended church together and were taught how anti-Christian they were. We were told that they couldn't have true morals or live a happy life because they didn't have a relationship with Jesus Christ. It made perfect sense to me. Our pastor warned us that atheists would attempt to steer us away from Jesus and were guided by Satan without their knowledge. We were advised to steer clear from them and avoid the temptation they would present.

Shortly after our mom's funeral, Brenda told me she doesn't believe in God. I didn't know how to react, and to be honest, I withdrew from contact with her, albeit unintentionally. I just felt awkward. I felt like everything we'd been through together, especially the passing of our parents, was clouded with lies. I felt betrayed in a way, because all of the exercises of comfort between us were centered around our religious beliefs and the knowledge that our parents were together again in God's kingdom.

After some time, we met for lunch and talked about the last 20 years – her time as an atheist. I realized that Brenda is still the same person I always knew her to be. She just had different beliefs than me about how the universe works. We've certainly disagreed about things before, but when it comes down to it, we're sisters, and we love and support each other. During our lunch date (that lasted upwards of six hours and turned into a dinner date as well), I learned a lot about my sister that I never knew. I learned that she felt out of place in our family for nearly 20 years, and hid her true self from us. I can only imagine that it must have been extremely difficult to feel like she couldn't be herself with her own family, for fear of being judged, ostracized, or even disowned by the people that were closest to her. I found out that the reaction I had to her atheism was exactly what she had feared would happen. I validated her decision to keep her atheism from our parents, knowing that their reaction would likely be more dramatic than mine.

After our meeting, I went home and broke down. I cried for her. I wasn't crying for her soul or reaching out to God to save her. I was crying because I felt foolish and misguided by my own pastor. I cried because I thought about how it must have been for her over the past 20 years, hiding her true identity from her family. I thought about the anguish she went through and the stress she must have been under to act like she still believed around us, but deep down was just going through the motions because she was scared.

I discovered that day that my sister hadn't changed. She was an atheist, but she was still the same moral, happy person I knew my whole life. She was moral and happy, not because she was raised Christian, but because her outlook on life changed. She still cared about other people and contributed to the lives of others because she cared about them in the present. I realized that the time I withdrew from Brenda, I was being foolish. I had plenty of friends that didn't hold the same beliefs as me. They weren't necessarily atheists, but they were Jewish, Muslim, other Christian denominations, or even Wiccan. And I didn't withdraw from them because of their beliefs. I figured, "to each his own" and certainly didn't consider them immoral or evil. So why did I have this reaction with my sister?

After some thought, I realized that it was because of what was drilled into me by our church. From my perspective, their approach to atheists was simply untrue. Atheists are people who just feel differently about my God, just like my other friends of different religions.

During our talk and ever since, my sister has not once attempted to steer me away from the Lord. She respects my right to believe what I want and doesn't try to interfere. That is proof to me that what was taught to us by our pastor is not true. If atheists are guided by Satan to steer us from God, then he's not doing such a good job with Brenda!

Now that we've cleared the air and can talk freely about religion when the topic comes up, we have an even closer relationship than we ever had. It turns out we weren't as close as we could have been, because she was always holding back a little bit due to her fears of how we'd react.

My advice to anyone going through this and feeling like they don't want to address the situation, is to do the exact opposite! Once you can talk freely about your differences, you'll see your relationships move to a whole new level. If you can open your heart and accept the atheist in your life as the person they are on the inside, then you will realize that they haven't changed. If there's one thing I've learned throughout this whole thing, it's that someone's religion (or lack of religion) does not define them. There are good and bad atheists, just as there are good and bad Christians. Everyone makes their own choices and should be judged by their actions, not by the philosophy that they think is true.

Mark A.
Jacksonville, Florida

I've been a Southern Baptist pastor for over 20 years, and for over five of those years, I thought I was a failure. In 2005, my only son, Daniel, then 17, informed me that he did not believe as I did. Worse yet, he was an atheist. I was overcome with sadness and a feeling of defeat. I was concerned for Daniel's soul. I was in fear of the community backlash once people in my own congregation heard of the news. If I could not lead my own son to salvation, then how could I lead my own congregation?

My initial reaction to the news was one of denial. I told him that this was a phase and that everyone questions their faith at some point. I prayed over him, referred him to some relevant Bible lessons, and tried to convince myself that I was right. In the next year or so, nothing had changed. He still identified himself as an atheist, but because we live in a deeply Christian community, Daniel wisely kept his atheism to himself. He understood the potential fallout that coming out to the rest of our family and his friends would cause. In order to give myself peace of mind that we would be protected from any backlash, I informed my son that if he was to continue to participate in our family, then he would need to keep his atheism under wraps. He was not to come out to anyone else.

Over the next four years, not much was said about Daniel's lack of belief, except for behind closed doors when my wife and I would pray for him when he wasn't present. He still went to church with the rest of the family, but not as regularly. When he was there, we could see that he mentally checked out. At family gatherings, especially ones of religious significance, Daniel participated, but rather unenthusiastically.

One day in 2010 I took a walk by myself. I wanted to have a talk with God. On that walk, I felt an overwhelming sense of guidance. I can only explain it to be God's intervention in my family life. This epiphany woke me up. God slapped me in the face and said "Be a father!" I realized that over the past 5 years of avoiding my son's loss of faith, I was denying my son as the person he is. I was only addressing the son I wanted him to be. What I didn't care to realize was that despite him not being a believer, he was still following Jesus' path. He was treating others with love. He was doing good in the community. As a father, there was plenty to be proud of.

I set up a family meeting and didn't inform anyone of the topic. Once we sat down, I told my son that I love him. I told him that I want him to be who he is, and that he was not to hide anything anymore. Daniel knew what I meant and his reaction was awesome. He immediately got up and hugged his mom and me with tears welling up in his eyes. At that point, I finally realized that this was what he wanted. He was tired of hiding but didn't want to do any harm to me or his family. He was a better son than I was a father. He showed me that an atheist could be a better leader than a Southern Baptist pastor, and in some ways, more Christ-like.

Since then, Daniel has not hidden his atheism. While I miss his presence at church, I'm proud that he has continued on his own path. It's a difficult pill to swallow at times, but I know that he's a good man, and if the Lord I know meets him one day, Daniel will be rewarded for his righteous path, regardless of his religious affiliation.

We are once again able to have open, honest communication, and Daniel's perspective on issues concerning religion is one of our favorite things to hear. We have great discussions about religion, made even more interesting by his contributions. No one tries to convert or "de-convert" each other, but instead, we show respect for each other's beliefs and views.

I no longer feel like a failure because Daniel exhibits Christian qualities every day. There are plenty of people in my congregation who worship on Sunday and sin on Monday. Daniel skips the worship, but sets a terrific example every day of the week.

Linda R.
St. Paul, Minnesota

My husband is an atheist. It took me a long time to come to terms with that. He was raised Protestant, just as I was, and was involved in our church. That's where we met.

While dating, and into the early years of our marriage, we didn't talk about religion all that much. I never felt the need to, since having met him at a church function, I always thought I knew his feelings on it. But after we had our daughter, Jim sat me down and we had a long talk. He told me that he was involved in the church because he liked the sense of community it brought. He agreed with most of the moral teachings, but he didn't believe anything beyond that. He confessed that he never brought up the topic of religion because he never wanted to have the awkward conversation with me. But now that we had a daughter, he thought it was time. Being a doctor, he had a different view on life and death and everything that goes with it. He focused more on the natural world than, shall we say, the supernatural one. He didn't attribute great things to a higher power. He was an atheist.

He wanted to talk to me about it because he wanted to raise our daughter to think differently. He didn't want us to tell her what to believe; he wanted her to figure out what she believed on her own. He said he never had that opportunity, and felt that most religious people didn't either. That's why they believe what they do – because they were taught that way. After thinking about that for some time, I agreed with him. I was raised to believe certain things about God, just as everyone in my family was. It's just the way it was. I never questioned. In fact, I was told not to. Our talk didn't make me an atheist too, and that wasn't Jim's goal. He just wanted me to know what he thought and believed. I'm glad we had that talk though, because it helped me to examine some things. I do believe differently now, but in a better way. I actually think learning about my husband's atheism made me a better Christian.

For a while, I felt like I'd been lied to, but deep down I understood why. In another sense, I felt saddened because it was as if he was telling me that we'd be together on earth and not afterward. He was telling me he was an atheist, and from what I was taught, they don't go where I'm going when I die. So our death would be the last time we'll be together.

We talked about religion a lot after that, and I'm glad we did. If we hadn't, I'd be mourning every day for the rest of my life. I'd be forever sad that I'd be without my husband for eternity. There would be no solace.

That's because he died when our daughter was 4.

Had we not discussed it, and I shut him out, I wouldn't feel as I do now. I now believe that I'll see him again. Through our talks, we realized that if there is a God, and I believe there is, He knows what kind of man my Jim was. He was a caring father and doctor, spending years with the sick, working tirelessly to get them well again. He was a devoted husband and trusted member of our community. For that, he should be rewarded in Heaven.

I believe in a God who loves all of us and rewards us based on our actions, not based on whether or not we kneel down in front of an altar. So because of that, I believe I will see my husband again.

If I would have immediately judged Jim when he told me he was an atheist, I would still believe that he wasn't waiting for me, and I would live with that sorrow every day. Because I opened my mind and listened, I realized that nothing had changed. Jim was still the man I fell in love with, married, and had a beautiful daughter with. He wasn't inherently evil, just because he trusted his own critically thinking (God-given) brain, and decided for himself that he didn't believe in God. He wasn't doing evil. He was healing the sick, looking after his family, and doing good works with our church. Isn't that enough? It should be. It was for me.

I'd like to share with you a message to those who

refuse to discuss religion with their atheist loved ones:

Take the time to listen. Your son, daughter, husband, wife, cousin, brother, sister, or friend loves you. They deserve your ear. Show them that you respect them as a person enough to hear how they feel. We don't have to agree on this topic. All we have to do is understand each other and show love. Blocking someone out for being who they are is the worst thing a close friend or family member can do. Talk to your loved ones. Someday it will be too late.

ABOUT THE AUTHOR

Despite his Catholic upbringing and experience as a "saved" Christian in his early college years, Kevin came out as an atheist in the mid-1990s. A constitutional law enthusiast and advocate for separation of church and state, he now focuses on examining, explaining, and defending the Wall of Separation – especially in public school settings – through his writings and activism at SecularVoices.org.

Kevin is also the co-founder and Executive Director of Young Skeptics, an elementary-level after school program for kids, focused on critical thinking and evidence-based reasoning.

Kevin routinely delivers presentations to secular and religious local groups, at conferences, and at larger events such as the Reason Rally and the Ark Encounter Protest and Rally in 2016.

Kevin lives in Churchville, NY with his wife, Shannon, and sons, Ryan and Grayson. Aside from his activism and nonprofit work, his career resides in the corporate learning and development field.

Kevin can be found on Twitter (@SecularVoices) and Facebook (facebook.com/SecularVoicesOrg).

Please direct inquiries to kevin@secularvoices.org.

www.ingramcontent.com/pod-product-compliance
Lightning Source LLC
Chambersburg PA
CBHW061334040426
42444CB00011B/2910